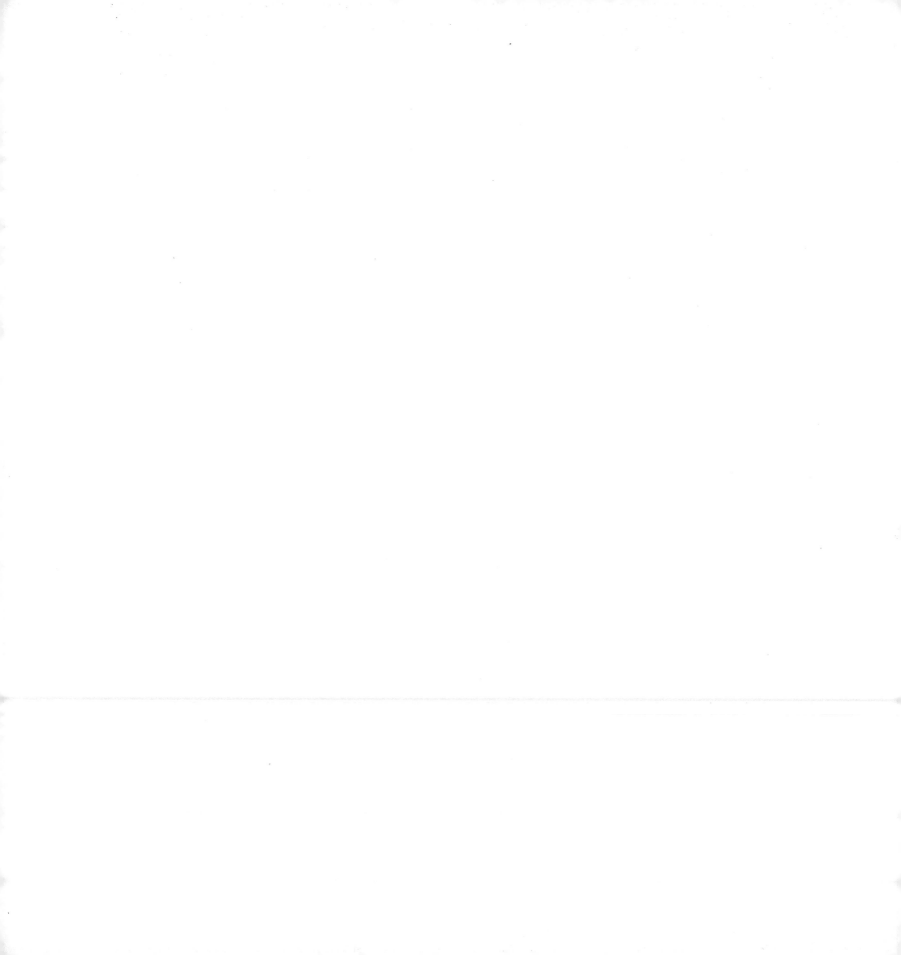

A Hui Hou
Until We Meet Again

Isabel, Hudson, and Adeline Bugge
with Ashley Bugge

Illustrated by Dawn Davidson

BROWN BOOKS KIDS

A Hui Hou
Until We Meet Again

Brown Books Publishing Group
Dallas, TX / New York, NY
www.BrownBooks.com
(972) 381-0009

A New Era in Publishing®

Publisher's Cataloging-In-Publication Data

Names: Bugge, Isabel, author. | Bugge, Hudson, author. | Bugge, Adeline, author. | Bugge, Ashley, author. | Davidson, Dawn (Dawn Doughty), 1977- illustrator.
Title: A hui hou : until we meet again / Isabel, Hudson, and Adeline Bugge ; with Ashley Bugge ; illustrated by Dawn Davidson.
Other Titles: Until we meet again
Description: Dallas, TX : Brown Books Publishing Group, [2020] | Interest age level: 003-006. | Summary: "Izzy, Hudson, and Addy lost their father in a terrible diving accident. Now they have to figure out how to accept his absence, live life without him, and make peace with missing him and carrying his memory forever. A Hui Hou: Until We Meet Again is a book for processing and understanding grief, told by children, to children, and for children"-- Provided by publisher.
Identifiers: ISBN 9781612544564
Subjects: LCSH: Bereavement in children--Juvenile literature. | Grief in children--Juvenile literature. | Fathers--Death--Juvenile literature. | Children and death--Juvenile literature. | CYAC: Bereavement. | Grief. | Fathers--Death. | Death.
Classification: LCC BF723.G75 B84 2020 | DDC [E] 155.937--dc23

ISBN 978-1-61254-456-4
LCCN 2020906269

Printed in Malaysia
10 9 8 7 6 5 4 3 2 1

For more information or to contact the author, please go to
www.AshleyBugge.com.

DEDICATION

This book is dedicated to our dad, Brian James Bugge.
We miss you and we love you, Dadda. A hui hou.

It's also dedicated to all of you who are missing your mom,
dad, or someone special too. We understand your sadness
and hope you realize you're not ever alone.

ACKNOWLEDGMENTS

First, we need to thank our dad, Brian James Bugge, for being the best dad in the entire world and for making sure we know how much he loved us.

We also want to thank our mom, Ashley Bugge, for helping us tell our story, for being super cool, and for taking us on lots of adventures. We love you, Mom!

To Brunella at the Military Editor Agency, for being relentless in your support and encouragement of our mom and us and for helping bring this book to life.

To Brown Books Publishing Group, for taking a chance on three young authors, for believing in this story, and for believing in us.

To Sara Macone, for braving Honolulu traffic on a rainy Hawaiian day to sit with us, hear our story, and agree to be our friend. We're grateful for you.

To Grandma Kasey, for showing up every Monday night and for loving us like you're really our grandma. We love you so much.

To NeeNee, Chananny, Kay, and V, thank you for all of the love and laughter. We wouldn't be who we are without each of you.

To Mama T, GPa, Ma, Grandpa, Aunt Nikki, Uncle Aaron, Uncle Zack, Aunt Kellie, Uncle Benny, Aunt Jenn, Aunt Jess, Aunt Aubrey, Uncle Brian, and all of our adopted aunties, uncles, friends, and cousins—especially our Hawaiian and PNW *ohana*—thank you for loving us and for your never-ending support.

Foreword

As a clinical psychologist, I am often called to help people of all ages face bereavement and grief. In the past fifteen years, I have worked in different environments—from hospital wards to private practices—and with many different individuals who have just experienced excruciatingly traumatic events. Given that people react to grief in different ways, I always adapt my approach to their own specific needs, offering varied coping strategies in order to facilitate the expression of their feelings.

Yet when it comes to helping people experiencing grief, there is one option that always seems to work better than the other ones: bibliotherapy. This term finds its etymological roots in ancient Greek: *biblion*, meaning "book," and *therapeía*, meaning "healing." Bibliotherapy invites people to express their feelings and, as a result, to begin their healing journey.

While adults have many different books to choose from when it comes to how to deal with grief, I have always found myself at odds with the very few options that children have. There are books that explain the meaning of mourning and death, which can be explained to young readers through different lenses, although mainly they are either philosophical or religious, since these books are written by psychologists, surviving parents, professional writers, or people of faith. Yet I have come across no book written from a child's point of view that explains what the experience of losing a parent at a very young age feels like.

What makes *A Hui Hou: Until We Meet Again* unique in its genre is that the main narrators are children speaking to other children. Isabel, Hudson, and Adeline don't offer any theories or doctrines—which are often quite far from a child's perception anyway. Reading this book, the little reader will meet vibrant words, honest feelings, and the raw emotions of children who have just lost their parent. It will be a disarming, lyrical, and anguishing encounter with their intrepid narration.

I met Ashley and her three children on a rainy Hawaiian day. I walked into that meeting knowing that I would meet personal sorrow, and I prepared myself mentally to help them through that. However, when I arrived, I was greeted by the happiest and most adorable family I had ever met! Isabel, Hudson, and Adeline shared a lot of information about themselves, their stuffed animals, and about each other. Hearing them talk so openly and honestly about their experience, I immediately thought that their mother's unique choice of allowing her children to narrate a book, giving their pain the spotlight and letting them spontaneously express grief in their own way by using their imaginations, was a winning strategy. While the children played together, I sat down with Ashley, and we started talking about her husband, Brian, the accident, the months that followed his death, and how this all led to this project: a book for children written by children.

When it comes to explaining death to children, some people turn to professional figures like myself; others turn to faith and religion, using concepts that might be too abstract for a young audience; others explain death using words that are too big for a child's vocabulary. This is why I find this book so extremely useful: it encourages a parent to begin the conversation with their child about what death is; it gives them tools to cope with the trauma; and provides children with the necessary vocabulary to address the traumatic event—especially because the book doesn't shy away from using words such as *death*. With the absence of an adult's filter, this book offers children the opportunity to understand death in a way that has not been explained before. No matter how young the reader is, children carry important feelings, thoughts, and information. They scrutinize the world around them, creating and sharing explanations, sometimes using illusions and imagination that make perfect sense in their world and help them cope with the traumatic situation they are in. As adults, we need to listen in silence. Let them lead and explain to us how to cope with those feelings and how to help them through the grieving process. This is a book for children written by children, and its authenticity can be found in the feelings and emotions of our little narrators.

I walked into that meeting as a clinical psychologist, but after meeting Ashley, Isabel, Hudson, and Adeline, I left as their friend. It was raining harder when I walked to my car, but a warm sun was shining bright in my heart.

Sara Macone, PsyD
Neuropsychologist and Cognitive Behavioral Therapist

Introduction

In May 2018, my three children lost the love, light, and hero of their lives. My husband, their father, passed away in a tragic scuba-diving accident while our family was stationed with the US Navy in Honolulu, Hawaii. This was never in our plan, never anything we imagined could happen to us as a family. As much as I wish this weren't their reality, our three children have had to live through it.

In the days, weeks, and months following their dad's death, I searched for books in this same realm that my kids could connect with. Something they could read and look at the pictures of to see that they were not alone, that other kids had been through something similar. I wasn't able to find anything depicting the tragedy my children had just endured—at least, not in a way that made sense to them. I found books with fuzzy animals talking to each other about being sad, and I found many books written by parents and psychologists talking about how children should feel, but nothing showing actual kids, like my own, who were working through this process.

And this is how this book came to be. A story written by children for children dealing with grief as they work through their own fears and emotions after losing a parent. The sights, sounds, ups, downs, and questions. All of it. My children use their own words to share their story, what they remember from the day of and days following their dad's death, and how they're able to make sense of it.

Rather than running away from their sadness or pretending like everything is OK when it isn't, they're now using their grief and their story to help others who find themselves in the same awful situation. As a family, we are rolling up our sleeves and confronting the grief head on, and we hope this book helps and inspires you and your family to do the same.

Ashley Bugge

Hi, I'm Isabel. My friends call me Izzy, so you can call me Izzy too.

This is my little brother, Hudson, and my baby sister, Adeline—we call her Addy.

Do you have a favorite toy?

My brother, Hudson, never
goes anywhere without his
favorite stuffed animal, Bear.

I'm a big girl, but I still have a favorite pink blanket I like to fall asleep with.

I think Addy is too little to have a favorite yet.

"Izzy, what about her little bear?"

"Hudson, shh!
I'm trying to tell a story."

Sorry about my little brother. He's still learning his manners.

Our dadda passed away a long time ago.

"We miss Dadda. He was so silly!"

Have you lost someone too?

We were in **HAWAII** when our dadda died.

We had been waiting in the car forever. Momma was crying and ran inside a building with bright red lights.

I thought that people must go there when they get hurt because there were doctors inside.

"Look, an ambulance!" I said. **"Hudson, cover your ears!"**

Do you like flashing lights?

Addy started crying. I thought she must be hungry.

Momma was inside the building for a long time. I wanted to go home.

I didn't like how that place made me feel.

"We're hooooome!"
Hudson cheered.

But Momma
seemed really sad.
I thought she must
need a hug.

**"Izzy, when is
Dadda coming home?"**
Hudson asked.

"I don't know, Hudson."

Dadda always came home for dinner when it was still blue outside. But it was getting dark. I hoped he would be home for dinner. I knew he would be really hungry!

I went to look out the window for him.

Momma said she needed to talk to us. She looked so sad. I squeezed her hand so she wouldn't be sad anymore.

"I want to sit next to Momma!" I said.

"Hudson, scoot over!"

When I was sad, my dadda told me that I'm super brave. I told Momma to be brave too.

Momma told us that Dadda swallowed too much water when he went scuba diving.

"Now he will be diving forever."

"Dadda loves diving!" Hudson said.

Momma said it was an accident. Dadda didn't mean to drink that much water. She said, "He wants to come home, but he can't. He passed away."

Drinking ocean water sounded icky. It's so salty!

Grandma and Grandpa came to visit.

For the next few days, a lot of people kept coming to visit us. I didn't know why they all looked so sad. Did they miss Dadda?

I was kind of sad too. I still really miss my dadda.

Our visitors brought us new toys.

"**Look, Izzy!**" Hudson told me.

"**Hudson, did you say thank you?**" I asked him.

"**Izzy, when's Dadda coming home?**" he wanted to know.
"**I want to show him my new train!**"

Dadda has been diving for many days now.

"Has it been forever yet?"

"No, Hudson. Forever is a reaaaally long time."

We went to Dadda's funeral. I liked the pretty dress I wore. Dadda would have liked it too. I spun around.

"Hudson, is Bear really brave like me?" I asked my brother.

"Oh, yes. And me, too, Izzy," he told me proudly.

I like to look at pictures of my dadda.
We had so many fun memories together.
There's a picture of Dadda on the stage.
The picture is from the day we went to
the beach and built sandcastles together.

In the picture, Dadda is smiling, and I want to smile back.
But sometimes, when I see it, I cry instead because I miss
him. Momma tells me it's OK to be sad.

I want to have a special picture of just me and Dadda to hang on my wall so I can remember him.

"Hudson and Addy, do you want one for your wall too?"

My favorite thing was when Dadda made me laugh.

What's your favorite memory of your dadda?

Hudson and Addy are so little, they keep asking when Dadda is coming home. "So Dadda can't come home?" they say. "Even if I miss him a whole lot?"

I'm the oldest and super brave, so I tell them he had an accident and can't come home, but we'll miss him forever. We look at pictures, and I tell them stories of how silly Dadda was.

I especially like to show Addy pictures of Dadda, because they make her happy, and I like to see her smile. Her giggles make me laugh!

"Da-Da!"

"Addy! That's right, this is our dadda!"

Addy is a baby, so she can't do much. She's not a good walker yet, but she's getting better every day.

I'm going to teach Addy all about Dadda.

Dadda used to tell me how all the animals in the ocean are our friends. His favorites were sea turtles, octopi, and dolphins.

But can I tell you a secret? I know Dadda's diving forever, but I'm scared for him to be in the ocean with some of those animals.

Today, Hudson, Addy, and I have to gift our leis to the ocean so we can say goodbye to Dadda. I tell them about it.

"Hudson, Addy, I want Dadda to get my flowers, but what if a shark gets them? What if Dadda gets eaten by a shark? I'm scared for him."

Then I imagine a shark out in the ocean. "Aloha!" he says.

"A shark!"
Hudson screams.

"Hudson, Addy, ruuuuuuun!"
I yell.

"Wait!" the shark tells us.
"I'm not here to hurt you."

"You're not?" I ask him.

"No, kids," he tells us. "I'm just here to tell you that you don't have to be scared for your dad. He's part of the ocean now, and we will look after him forever."

"You know my dadda?"
Hudson asks.

"Can you tell him we love him and we miss him?"

"Of course. And any time you miss him, you come to the ocean and look out here and know he loves and misses you too."

We love you, Dadda.

A HUI HOU.

About the Authors

We are Isabel, Hudson, and Adeline, and this is our story. We have been raised in a family of adventurers, and even though we've been through some really hard and scary times, we have been taught by our mom and dad—when he was alive—that it's OK to be scared, as long as we talk about it and find a way to get through it. So, we are writing this book to talk about it and work through it, and we hope to help inspire you to do the same.

We have had adventures all over the world (thirteen countries so far!), and we get excited when we learn about a place and then get to see it in real life. We don't like green vegetables, and we argue with each other sometimes, but we love PB&J and singing along to the songs of *Moana*, which remind us of our home in Hawaii. We love playing outside—especially at the beach—and we love being on the water, just like our mom and dad. We also think we're hilarious.

Our mom, Ashley Bugge, has written a couple of books. If you want to read more about us, our dad, or how our family pulled through overwhelming tragedy, you can do so at www.AshleyBugge.com. You can also follow us on Instagram for updates about our latest adventures @Ashley.Bugge or @TheBuggeBabies or on Facebook at www.Facebook.com/TheBuggeBabies.

About the Illustrator

Dawn Davidson is a freelance artist in Winter Garden, Florida. A lover of great children's literature, she is inspired by the classical illustrators of the past and strives to achieve a sense of timelessness by mimicking traditional media in her digital work. Combining classical drawing skills, vibrant color use, and a sense of playful whimsy to create memorable characters and humorous compositions, she enjoys nothing more than to bring a story to life through beautiful, engaging art. She loves family, travel, Celtic mythology, period and fantasy costuming, and dreaming of retiring to a mountain cottage in a state that has seasons.